My Little Book of
Tractors

by Rod Green

Quarto is the authority on a wide range of topics.

Quarto educates, entertains and enriches the lives of our readers—enthusiasts and lovers of hands-on living.

www.quartoknows.com

Publisher: Maxime Boucknooghe
Editorial Director: Victoria Garrard
Art Director: Miranda Snow
Design and editorial: Tall Tree Ltd

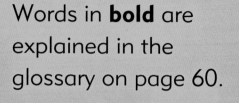

Words in **bold** are explained in the glossary on page 60.

First published in the UK in 2016 by
QED Publishing
Part of the Quarto Group
The Old Brewery, 6 Blundell Street, London N7 9BH

www.quartoknows.com/brand/979/QED-Publishing/

A catalogue record for this book is available from the British Library

ISBN 978 1 78493 471 2

Printed in China

Contents

The modern tractor

Tractors of different types have been used on farms for more than 200 years, and farmers today rely on the modern tractor to do all sorts of jobs.

>> This tractor is pulling a hay rake that sorts hay into neat rows.

∀ Some tractors have a roll bar to protect the driver should the tractor tip over. Others have enclosed cabs.

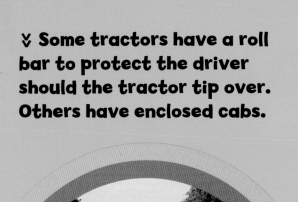

Tractors have wide wheels that spread their weight and stop them sinking into soft ground. The tyres have deep, chunky **treads** to give them good **grip**.

∀ The driver sits in the middle of the tractor. This helps him steer straight across a field.

Steam power

Before there were tractors, horses were used to pull **ploughs**. That began to change when the steam engine was invented early in the 19th century.

>> Pulling a plough was hard work for horses, but easy for a steam engine.

By 1850, steam engines placed at the side of a field could use cables to drag a plough across the field. Unlike horses, the steam engine never grew tired or needed to rest.

⋁This engine has its chimney folded ready to be transported. It has wheels but was still pulled by a horse.

Traction engines

⌄ This engine has a roof to keep the rain off.

Traction engines first appeared in the 1860s. These were powered by steam, not pulled by horses.

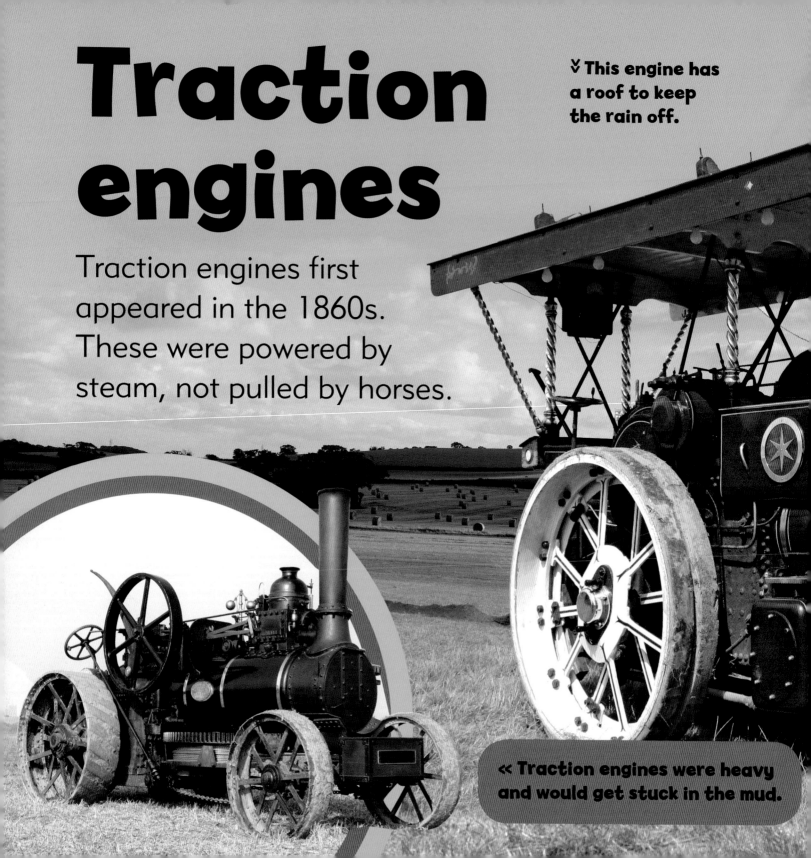

« Traction engines were heavy and would get stuck in the mud.

Traction means 'pulling'. It is from the word 'traction' that the modern tractor gets its name.

⌃ A traction engine's steering wheel steered the front wheels, just like a modern tractor.

Petrol engines

By the beginning of the 20th century, **petrol** engines were being used to power tractors.

˅ The Ivel of 1902 was the first successful petrol-engined tractor.

⌃ Early tractors had metal or wooden treads instead of rubber tyres.

Petrol engines were lighter than steam engines. A petrol tractor could drive across a field without sinking in and damaging the field. This meant that a petrol tractor could pull a plough across a field.

THE IVEL

>> By the 1940s tractors had smaller petrol engines. They also had rubber tyres.

Two-wheel tractors

Tractors with two wheels are sometimes called walking tractors because the driver walks behind.

>> This farmer in Thailand is using a walking tractor in his rice field. Rice is grown in flooded fields.

<< A walking tractor can pull a trailer. The driver sits on the trailer.

« Controls for the engine and the brakes are on the handlebars of this early walking tractor.

Walking tractors were invented at the beginning of the 20th century and are still in use today.

Four-wheel tractors

Most tractors have four wheels. The rear wheels are often much bigger than the front wheels.

^ **This tractor has** all-wheel drive and large wheels at the back and the front.

>> **Smaller front wheels make a tractor easier to steer.**

Tractors with larger rear wheels usually have rear-wheel drive. This means that the engine powers the rear wheels. Big rear wheels grip the ground better.

>> **This early tractor has metal spikes on its rear wheels that help it to grip soft ground.**

Multi-wheel tractors

Heavy tractors have lots of wheels. Extra wheels spread the tractor's weight across the ground to stop the tractor sinking in.

˅ **Six wheels give this tractor good grip, and it is narrow enough to drive on roads.**

∨ With eight wheels, this tractor is too wide to drive on normal roads.

≪ All of the front wheels turn in order to steer an eight-wheel tractor.

Tractors with lots of wheels and all-wheel drive can pull bigger, heavier equipment. Large fields can be ploughed much faster.

On the farm

Farm tractors have lots of jobs to do in the farmyard as well as in the fields.

Farmers use tractors for towing trailers, lifting heavy loads and transporting them around even the muddiest areas of the farm.

>> This tractor has a claw to lift hay bales and a long arm to stack them very high.

<< Towing a light trailer carrying bales of hay is easy work for this tractor.

>> Links to attach trailers or equipment are between the tractor's rear wheels.

In the fields

Tractors can work in the most difficult conditions. This allows farmers to work in all weathers.

⌃ Tractors can deliver hay to feed cattle or sheep, even in deep snow.

« This tractor is ploughing a rice field. Nets protect the driver from insects.

Farmers must sometimes work all through the night to harvest a crop before rain or cold weather can ruin it. Tractors get the job done quickly.

⌃ At night farmers use the tractor's powerful lights to see the field and to check their equipment.

Combine harvesters

Combine harvesters are special tractors used to cut a crop like wheat or barley. They then separate the **grain** from the rest of the plant.

<< **The large wheels are at the front to spread the weight of the** header **that cuts the crop.**

Combine harvesters are often used in teams of two or more. This helps harvest the crop quickly before wind, rain or cold can spoil it.

⌃ **The grain is gathered in a** hopper **on the back of the combine harvester.**

>> A full hopper is emptied into a chaser bin towed by a normal tractor.

Crop pickers

Tractors are used to harvest many different crops. Some are specially built for the task.

⌄ Grapes are picked from vines. The crop-picking tractor's wheels go either side of the vine.

« A tractor pulling chaser bins collects grapes picked by the special tractor.

Tractors used for picking grapes or cotton must do so without harming the plant. The plant will then produce another crop the following year.

>> **The cotton picked by this harvester is fed into a hopper behind the driver.**

Row crop tractors

Row crop tractors have wheels that go between rows of plants without damaging them.

« This tractor is towing a baler. A baler makes crops into neat bundles.

<< An early three-wheeled row crop tractor.

The first row crop tractors had just three wheels. This made them easy to steer between rows, but the tractors could tip over on steep slopes. Tractors with four wheels do not tip over so easily.

<< Tractors spray crops to kill insects that would destroy the plants.

Power tools

Tractors can be used to provide power for tools or equipment. The power comes from the tractor's engine.

» This tractor is powering a pump to spray water out of a ditch. The spray is watering the field.

Tractors can use tools such as digger buckets in front. The engine can also power equipment attached between the back wheels.

⌄ **This tractor is used in** construction. **It has a digger bucket at the front and a road drill at the rear.**

« **The pump attached to the rear of this tractor has pipes to take water from a pond to the fields.**

Loaders

Loaders are used for loading other vehicles. Loaders can lift large, heavy objects.

˅ **Loading heavy hay bales onto a trailer is a simple job for this tractor.**

˄ **This tractor has a** telescopic **loading arm. The arm can extend to reach up to seven metres.**

Loader tractors are used on farms, in **factories**, in **warehouses** and on construction sites. The loading equipment is in front so that the driver can see where he is putting the load.

« The bucket of this quarry loader can lift around 15 tonnes of rock. That's the weight of two elephants.

Diggers

The powerful engines of tractors make them excellent at digging rock or soil.

⩔ **This quarry digger's bucket has strong teeth for scraping up rocks.**

A tractor with an **excavator** arm can be used to dig a ditch or knock down a tree. Larger, more powerful diggers can knock down buildings.

« A digger arm can be powered from the rear of a tractor.

» This tractor is towing a scraper. The scraper removes the top layer of soil.

Hedgerows and forests

Tractors stop hedges from growing over country roads. They also help to deal with the mightiest trees in the forest.

« This tractor is using a hedge trimming tool on a country road.

>> Powerful steel jaws are used to carry massive logs.

<< A tractor uses a tool like a claw to load logs onto its trailer.

Tractors are ideal for forestry work. They can drive over the roughest forest tracks, tow logs to the nearest road and then load them onto trucks.

Snow ploughs and blowers

In the winter, cars and trucks can slip and slide on snowy roads. Tractors can come to the rescue.

« The blade tool used by this tractor pushes snow aside. It is called a snow plough.

Tractors can use all-wheel drive and their chunky tyres to drive on snow without skidding. This makes them ideal for clearing snow.

⌄ **The snow blower on this tractor scoops up snow and blows it away from the road.**

» **A walking tractor with a snow blower is used to clear pavements.**

Gun tractors

Tractors with **caterpillar tracks** were first used in muddy forests. These tractors went into battle in the **First World War**.

« Tanks like this were first used in battle by the British Army in 1916.

>> A First World War tractor with caterpillar tracks tows a British Army field gun in deep mud.

Heavy field guns were towed by horses, but horses often got stuck in the mud. Tractors with caterpillar tracks were used instead. This gave inventors the idea for the first tanks.

⋀ **This Sherman tank from 1942 was used during the** Second World War. **It looks more like a modern tank.**

Bulldozers

Bulldozers are extremely heavy. They have caterpillar tracks and make very powerful tractors.

>> **This bulldozer has a rear digging tool to rip up uneven ground. The front blade scoops up the soil or flattens it out.**

Bulldozers are used to scrape and flatten bumpy ground so that it can be built on. They are also tough enough to knock down houses.

^ **The blade on this bulldozer is scraping up soil to be flattened.**

^ **Bulldozers fitted with buckets can pile rocks and soil into mounds.**

Snow tractors

Tractors with caterpillar tracks can be driven over deep snow. They don't sink in or skid.

⌃ These special Ferguson tractors were used to cross the Antarctic in 1957.

Wide caterpillar tracks give snow tractors enough grip to drive up steep mountain slopes. Cabs keep the drivers warm even in the coldest weather.

« This machine is like a snow bulldozer. It is used to flatten the snow on ski slopes.

» This snow tractor can float and uses its tracks to swim through water.

43

Farm tractors with tracks

Caterpillar tracks are sometimes used on farm tractors. They stop the heaviest machines sinking into soft ground.

» This tractor uses its bucket wheel for digging ditches on a sugar plantation in Hawaii.

<< The front wheels of this 1940s tractor were outside the tracks so that they could be used for steering.

Most tractors with tracks are steered by slowing or stopping the tracks on one side. This makes the tractor turn towards that side.

Bucket wheel

⋏ Large modern tractors may have tracks instead of using eight wheels.

Military tractors

Military forces need tractors to tow, load and dig.

Military tractors used in battle have **armour** to protect the driver from bullets and bombs. They are used for digging trenches, building defences and clearing obstacles from roads.

⌃ The two bombs this tractor is carrying weigh more than a large car.

>> Battlefield tractors need all-wheel drive to power safely through mud.

« A tractor dumps gravel in a river to create a ford for other vehicles.

47

Small tractors

Small tractors are used in places where there is not enough space for a big tractor to move about. They are perfect for gardens.

« Small tractors are used to clear snow from footpaths.

They may not be big, but small tractors are still powerful enough to pull or lift heavy loads. Some also have caterpillar tracks.

⌃ A tractor like this can lift around 900 kilos in its bucket. That's the weight of two racehorses.

« This garden tractor is being used to mow grass. These are sometimes called 'ride-on mowers'.

Giant tractors

Some farm tractors are huge, but the biggest tractors of all are used in mines and quarries.

The largest tractors are bucket excavators used in mining. Some are almost 100 metres tall and need at least five people to control them.

⌄ **This farm tractor's engine is ten times as big as an average car engine.**

>> This massive farm tractor has a ladder for the driver to reach his cab.

⌄ Bucket excavators move very slowly on twelve sets of caterpillar tracks.

Excavators

Excavators are special tractors used for digging. They are often used on building sites.

The top half of an excavator can turn to face any direction. The digging arm can take soil or rock from one side and load it into a truck on the other.

>> An excavator loads rocks in a quarry.

>> If there isn't room for a big digger, a mini excavator can do the job.

>> This excavator has wheels instead of tracks and is digging salt.

Airport tractors

Tractors have a number of jobs to do at an airport, including towing aircraft.

A blast from an aircraft's jet engines could damage airport buildings. To avoid this, aircraft are towed or pushed by pushback tractors when close to buildings.

⌄ Pushback tractors are flat and low to fit beneath an aircraft.

« A tractor pulls a train of trailers full of baggage.

IBHAYI

SAK

>> **This tractor has a** conveyor belt **for loading baggage and cargo.**

Emergency tractors

Tractors are used by the emergency services
for jobs that other vehicles would find difficult.

As they can pull heavy loads and drive in snow,
mud or even water, tractors are valuable vehicles
for the emergency services.

**« This snow tractor is
used as an ambulance
on the steep slopes of
mountain ski resorts.**

⌄Tractors can wade into the sea to launch and recover a lifeboat.

⌃ Police officers use tractors to teach the public about crime in the countryside.

BRIDLINGTON LIFEBOAT

Competition tractors

Tractors are hard-working machines, but they can also be used in competitions.

« Tractor races are held in muddy fields.

˅ This monster tractor uses the pulling power of three engines.

Tractors compete in pulling competitions. They must pull a sled down a track that is 100 metres long.

>> The sled this tractor is pulling can weigh up to 29 tonnes – as much as seven hippos.

Glossary

all-wheel drive When a vehicle's engine supplies power to all of its wheels, instead of just the front or rear wheels.

armour A strong material that is used as protection from bullets or bombs.

bale A large, neat bundle of hay or cotton.

caterpillar tracks Belts looped around the wheels of off-road vehicles. Tracks provide grip and spread the vehicle's weight to stop it sinking in soft ground.

construction A term describing the tasks involved in creating or building something.

conveyor belt A moving belt that transports items from one end of the belt to the other.

excavator Excavate means to dig, and an excavator is a digger.

factories Manufactured goods like cars, toys and clothes are made in factories.

field gun A large battlefield weapon that fires over long distances.

First World War A war that involved most countries between 1914 and 1918.

ford A shallow part of a river used as a crossing point.

grain Seeds harvested to be eaten by humans or animals.

grip The force of a vehicle's wheels pushing on the ground.

hay Cut grass that is dried and used to feed livestock.

header A cutting tool powered by a tractor and used to harvest crops.

hopper A large container used to collect and transport grain or other crops.

petrol A fuel made from oil.

plough A blade-like tool that cuts into soil and turns it over.

quarry A place where useful rocks, such as slate, are dug from the ground.

Second World War A war that involved most countries between 1939 and 1945.

telescopic Something that can be extended like a telescope.

treads The grooves and ridges on wheels and tyres.

vines Climbing or creeping plants. Some produce grapes and are grown as crops.

warehouse A building used for storage.

Index

Picture credits